THE ROUGH FIELD
1961-1971

I had never known sorrow,
Now it is a field I have inherited, and I till it.

from the Afghan

The Greeks say it was the Turks who burned down
Smyrna. The Turks say it was the Greeks. Who will
discover the truth?
The wrong has been committed.
The important thing is who will redeem it?

George Seferis

the rough field

OLD MOULDS ARE BROKEN IN THE NORTH

IN THE DARK STREETS FIRING STARTS . . . .

JOHN MONTAGUE

WAKE FOREST UNIVERSITY PRESS

Wake Forest University Press

This sixth American edition of *The Rough Field* has been corrected and reprinted based on the designs by Liam Miller for the first and the third Irish editions.

First edition 1972
Second edition 1974
Third edition 1979
Fourth edition 1984
Fifth edition 1989
Sixth edition, with revised notes, 2005

Printed in the United States of America
Library of Congress Control Number: 2004117259

ISBN 1-930630-21-2

CONTENTS

PREFACE

This poem begins in the early Sixties, when I went to Belfast
to receive a small poetry prize, the first, I think, to exist in
that part of the world. (Ironically, the Irish papers hailed it as
'Dublin Poet wins Belfast Prize', so little were they accus-
tomed to a poet of my background.) To deepen the paradox,
the award was presented in the Assembly Rooms of the
Presbyterian Church in Belfast, a drab Victorian building in
the heart of the city. And as 'Like Dolmens round my
Childhood' was being read, I heard the rumble of drums,
preparing for 'the Twelfth', the annual Orange festival.

Bumping down towards Tyrone a few days later by bus, I
had a kind of vision, in the medieval sense, of my home area,
the unhappiness of its historical destiny. And of all such
remote areas where the presence of the past was compounded
with a bleak economic future, whether in Ulster, Brittany or
the Highlands of Scotland. I managed to draft the opening
and the close, but soon realised that I did not have the
technique for so varied a task. Although living in Berkeley
introduced me to the debate on open-form from *Paterson*,
through Olson, to Duncan, I was equally drawn by rooted
poets like MacDiarmid in *A Drunk Man*. . . . At intervals
during the decade I returned to it, when the signs seemed
right. An extreme Protestant organisation put me on its
mailing list, for instance, and the only antidote I could find
against such hatred was to absorb it into 'The Bread God.'
And ten years later I was given another small award, again
from the North, to complete the manuscript.

Although as the Ulster crisis broke, I felt as if I had been
stirring a witch's cauldron, I never thought of the poem as
tethered to any particular set of events. One explores an
inheritance to free oneself and others, and if I sometimes saw
the poem as taking over where the last bard of the O'Neills
left off, the New Road I describe runs through Normandy as
well as Tyrone. And experience of agitations in Paris and
Berkeley taught me that the violence of disputing factions is
more than a local phenomenon. But one must start from
home — so the poem begins where I began myself, with a
Catholic family in the townland of Garvaghey, in the county
of Tyrone, in the province of Ulster.

1989

I

HOME AGAIN

Lost in our separate work
We meet at dusk in a narrow lane.
I press back against a tree
To let him pass, but he brakes
Against our double loneliness
With: 'So you're home again!'

I

Vast changes have taken place,
and rulers have passed away,
dynasties fallen, since that
glorious autumn day when Lord
Mountjoy, accompanied by his
land steward, arrived by coach
in Omagh . . .

> *Catching a bus at Victoria Station,*
> Symbol of Belfast in its iron bleakness,
> We ride through narrow huckster streets
> (Small lamps bright before the Sacred Heart
> Bunting tagged for some religious feast)
> To where Cavehill and Divis, stern presences,
> Brood over a wilderness of cinemas and shops,
> Victorian red-brick villas, framed with aerials,
> Bushmill hoardings, Orange and Legion Halls.
> A fringe of trees affords some ease at last
> From all this dour, despoiled inheritance,
> The shabby through-otherness of outskirts:
> 'God is Love', chalked on a grimy wall
> Mocks a culture where constraint is all.

His Lordship stood high with
the government of the day. He
was wealthy and had acquired,
through Charles Blount, the
first Earl, an immense tract of
the O'Neill country. As he rode
along no menacing banner of
that ancient sept frowned down
on him from dun or tower.

> Through half of Ulster that Royal Road ran
> Through Lisburn, Lurgan, Portadown,
> Solid British towns, lacking local grace.
> Headscarved housewives in bulky floral skirts
> Hugged market baskets on the rexine seats
> Although it was near the borders of Tyrone —
> End of a Pale, beginning of O'Neill —
> Before a stranger turned a friendly face,
> Yarning politics in Ulster monotone.
> Bathos as we bumped all that twilight road,

Tales of the Ancient Order, Ulster's Volunteers:
Narrow fields wrought such division,
And narrow they were, though as darkness fell
Ruled by the evening star, which saw me home

Hugh O'Neill was soundly
asleep by the banks of the
Tiber, where no bugle blast of
his fiery clansmen could ever
reach or rouse him. McArt's
stronghold was a mere tradition
by the banks of the Strule.
His Lordship could ride easily
for the echoes of Lamh Dearg
Abus had long since faded
away among the hills of the
north. . . .

'Broken was Tirowen's pride,
And vanquished Clanaboy.'
Ulster Herald

To a gaunt farmhouse on this busy road,
Bisecting slopes of plaintive moorland,
Where I assume old ways of walk and work
So easily, yet feel the sadness of return
To what seems still, though changing.
No Wordsworthian dream enchants me here
With glint of glacial corrie, totemic mountain,
But merging low hills and gravel streams,
Oozy blackness of bog-banks, pale upland grass;
Rough Field in the Gaelic and rightly named
As setting for a mode of life that passes on:
Harsh landscape that haunts me,
Well and stone, in the bleak moors of dream.
With all my circling a failure to return.

2

Hearing the cock crow in the dark,
The first thing to move in the desolate farmyard,
I lay awake to listen, the tripled shrill calls
As jagged and shill as water
While a pale movement of dawn
Began to climb and outline
The dark window frame.

Those were my first mornings
Fresh as Eden, with dew on the face,
Like first kiss, the damp air:
On dismantled flagstones,
From ash-smoored embers
Hands now strive to rekindle
That once leaping fire.

3

On the recommendation of the Earl
of Belmore, H.M.L., the Lord
Chancellor has appointed the
following gentlemen to the
Commission of the peace of
Tyrone County; on behalf and
under the Seal of H.M. Queen
Victoria: Dr. J. J. Todd, Omagh;
William Anderson, The Grange,
Tullyhogue; Neil Bradley,
Strabane; Robert Hall Anderson,
Sixmilecross; John Montague,
Garvaghey.

Between small, whin-tough hills,
The first slated house in the district;
Garvaghey, with its ring of firs.
From a silvered daguerrotype
My grandfather, country lawyer,
Hedge schoolmaster, Redmondite
Stares out, white beard curled
Like a seahorse. Hovering anonymous
In the background, his patient
Tight corsetted wife prepares
Another meal to absorb the spirit
That stokes a patriarch's wit.
The children are kept out of sight,
All eight surviving; she'll die
With the eleventh.
                    Such posed
Conceit recalls post Famine years
When Catholics regain the precious
Right to rise above their neighbours.

[12]

Labourers stooped in his fields while
John Montague presided at Petty Sessions
Or attended meetings of a Belfast firm.
Sundays, rattling the leather reins,
He drove a side-car over the Fox's leap
To the dark glens of Altamuskin
Where the Tagues came from. A blend
Of wild Irish and Ulster Puritan —
The dram of poteen beside Cardinal Manning
In his bedroom — combine to make
A rustic gentleman.

                              Sixty years
Later, his succession was broken,
Sons scattered to Australia, Brooklyn.
The rotting side-car propped a hole
In the hedge, box lanterns askew.
All the sadness of a house in decay
Showed in the weed-grown cobbles,
The gaping stables. But the stacks
Still rode the stone circled haggard
And the tall shed was walled high
And dry with turf, for the war years.
Then the wide tent of a hearth
Where Dagda's cauldron swung
Shrank to a coal-fired stove
And tiled stone.

4

My uncle played the fiddle — more elegantly, the violin —
A favourite at barn and cross roads dance,
He knew *The Morning Star* and *O'Neill's Lament*.

Bachelor head of a house full of sisters,
Runner of poor racehorses, spendthrift,
He left for the New World in an old disgrace.

He left his fiddle in the rafters
When he sailed, never played afterwards,
A rural art silenced in the discord of Brooklyn.

[13]

A heavily-built man, tranquil-eyed as an ox,
He ran a wild speakeasy, and died of it.
During the Depression many dossed in his cellar.

I attended his funeral in the Church of the Redemption,
Then, unexpected successor, reversed time
To return where he had been born.

During my schooldays the fiddle rusted
(The bridge fell away, the catgut snapped)
Reduced to a plaything, stinking of stale rosin.

The country people asked if I also had music
(All the family had had) but the fiddle was in pieces
And the rafters remade, before I discovered my craft.

Twenty years afterwards, I saw the church again,
And promised to remember my burly godfather
And his rural craft, after this fashion:

So succession passes, through strangest hands.

5

Like dolmens round my childhood, the old people.

Jamie MacCrystal sang to himself
A broken song, without tune, without words;
He tipped me a penny every pension day,
Fed kindly crusts to winter birds.
When he died his cottage was robbed,
Mattress and money box torn and searched,
Only the corpse they didn't disturb.

Maggie Owens was surrounded by animals,
A mongrel bitch and shivering pups,
Even in her bedroom a she-goat cried,
She was a well of gossip defiled,
Fanged chronicler of a whole countryside;
Reputed a witch, all I could find
Was her lonely need to deride.

The Nialls lived along a mountain lane
Where heather bells bloomed, clumps of foxglove.
All were blind, with Blind Pension and Wireless.
Dead eyes serpent-flickered as one entered
To shelter from a downpour of mountain rain.
Crickets chirped under the rocking hearthstone
Until the muddy sun shone out again.

Mary Moore lived in a crumbling gatehouse
Famous as Pisa for its leaning gable.
Bag apron and boots, she tramped the fields
Driving lean cattle from a miry stable.
A by-word for fierceness, she fell asleep
Over love stories, Red Star and Red Circle,
Dreamed of gypsy love rites, by firelight sealed.

Wild Billy Eagleson married a Catholic servant girl
When all his loyal family passed on:
We danced round him shouting 'To hell with King Billy'
And dodged from the arc of his flailing blackthorn.
Forsaken by both creeds, he showed little concern
Until the Orange drums banged past in the summer
And bowler and sash aggressively shone.

Curate and doctor trudged to attend them,
Through knee-deep snow, through summer heat,
From main road to lane to broken path,
Gulping the mountain air with painful breath.
Sometimes they were found by neighbours,
Silent keepers of a smokeless hearth,
Suddenly cast in the mould of death.

Ancient Ireland, indeed! I was reared by her bedside,
The rune and the chant, evil eye and averted head,
Fomorian fierceness of family and local feud.
Gaunt figures of fear and of friendliness,
For years they trespassed on my dreams,
Until once, in a standing circle of stones,
I felt their shadows pass

Into that dark permanence of ancient forms.

II

THE LEAPING FIRE

I. M. BRIGID MONTAGUE (1876–1966)

Each morning, from the corner
of the hearth, I saw a miracle
as you sifted the smoored ashes
to blow

       a fire's sleeping remains
back to life, holding the burning brands
of turf, between work hardened hands.
I draw on that fire. . . .

I

The Little Flower's Disciple

Old lady, I now celebrate
to whom I owe so much;
bending over me in darkness
a scaly tenderness of touch

skin of bony arm & elbow
sandpapered with work:
because things be to be done
and simplicity did not shirk

the helpless, hopeless task
of maintaining a family farm,
which meant, by legal fiction,
maintaining a family name.

The thongless man's boots,
the shapeless bag apron:
would your favourite saint
accept the harness of humiliation

you bore constantly until
the hiss of milk into the pail
became as lonely a prayer as
your vigil at the altar rail.

Roses showering from heaven
upon Her uncorrupted body
after death, celebrated
the Little Flower's sanctity

& through the latticed grill
of your patron's enclosed order
an old French nun once threw me
a tiny sack of lavender.

So from the pressed herbs
of your least memory, sweetness exudes:
that of the meek and the selfless,
who should be comforted.

[18]

2

Nightly she climbs the
narrow length of the stairs
to kneel in her cold room
as if she would storm
heaven with her prayers

which, if they have power,
now reach across the quiet
night of death to where
instead of a worn rosary,
I tell these metal keys.

The pain of a whole family
she gathers into her hands:
the pale mother who died
to give birth to children
scattered to the four winds

who now creakingly arouse
from darkness, distance
to populate the corners
of this silent house
they once knew so well.

A draught whipped candle
magnifies her shadow —
a frail body grown monstrous,
sighing in a trance
before the gilt crucifix —

& as the light gutters
the shadows gather to dance
on the wall of the next room
where, a schoolboy searching sleep,
I begin to touch myself.

The sap of another generation
fingering through a broken tree
to push fresh branches
towards a further light,
a different identity.

[19]

3

Your white hair
on the thin rack
of your shoulders

it is hard to
look into the eyes
of the dying

who carry away
a part of oneself —
a shared world

& you, whose life
was selflessness,
now die slowly

broken down by
process to a pale
exhausted beauty

the moon in her
last phase, caring
only for herself.

I lean over the
bed but you barely
recognize me &

when an image
forces entry —
Is that John?

Bring me home
you whimper &
I see a house

shaken by traffic
until a fault runs
from roof to base

[20]

but your face has
already retired into
the blind, animal

misery of age
paying out your
rosary beads

hands twitching
as you drift
towards nothingness

4

Family legend held
that this frail
woman had heard
the banshee's wail

& on the night
she lay dying
I heard a low,
constant crying

over the indifferent
roofs of Paris —
the marsh bittern
or white owl sailing

from its foul
nest of bones
to warn me with
a hollow note

& among autobuses
& taxis, the shrill
paraphernalia of a
swollen city

I crossed myself
from rusty habit
before I realised
why I had done it.

A hollow note.

III

THE BREAD GOD

A COLLAGE OF RELIGIOUS MISUNDERSTANDINGS

FOR THOMAS MONTAGUE, S.J.,
ON HIS EIGHTIETH BIRTHDAY

I break again into the lean parish of my art
Where huddled candles flare before a shrine
And men with caps in hand kneel stiffly down
To see the many-fanged monstrance shine.

The Prime Minister, 10 Downing Street, London

Dear Sir:
    We take the liberty of writing to you on the serious subject of the proposed entry of Great Britain into Europe. After lengthy and serious discussions we have resolved to bring to your attention some constitutional issues which *must* be settled before the Government or the Sovereign can hand over their powers to an Assembly of Europe.
    (1) The Commonwealth countries would still have a head of state, who would be subordinate to such Assembly should Her Majesty sign 'The Treaty of Rome'. . . .
    (2) We fail to see how Her Majesty could be advised to sign away Her powers to an assembly, the membership of which is composed of people not of the Reformed Faith. What happens to the Coronation Oath?
    . . . until a mandate is sought on these issues, we intend to take all possible constitutional action to prevent the Government from signing 'The Treaty of Rome'. We are currently studying the legal avenues with the view of obtaining an injunction against the British Government to prevent it from taking the United Kingdom into the European Common Market.

The Belfast County Grand Lodge
Independent Loyal Orange Institution of Ireland

*He who stood at midnight upon a little mount which rose behind
the chapel, might see between five and six thousand torches, all
blazing together, and forming a level mass of red dusky light, burn-
ing against the dark horizon. These torches were so close to each other
that their light seemed to blend, as if they had constituted one wide
surface of flame; and nothing could be more preternatural-looking
than the striking and devotional countenance of those who were
assembled at their midnight worship, when observed beneath this
canopy of fire. . . .*

Lights outline a hill   Christmas Morning
As silently the people,
Like shepherd and angel
On that first morning,
March from Altcloghfin,
Beltany, Rarogan,
Under rimed hawthorn,
Gothic evergreen,
Grouped in the warmth
& cloud of their breath,
Along cattle paths
Crusted with ice,
Tarred roads to this
Gray country chapel
Where a gas-lamp hisses
To light the crib
Under the cross-beam's
Damp flaked message:
GLORIA IN EXCELSIS.

*Yes, I remember Carleton's description of Christmas in Tyrone,
but things had changed at the end of the century. Religion was at
a pretty low ebb in those days. We had one Mass at 10 o'clock on
Sundays at which a handful went to communion. We went to
confession and communion about every four months. The priests
did not take much interest in the people and did not visit them
except for sick calls. I think I became a priest because we were the
most respectable family in the parish and it was expected of me,
but what I really wanted to do was to join the army, which was out
of the question. So you see how your uncle became a Jesuit!*

Christmas, Melbourne, 1960.

[25]

Hesitant step of a late-comer.
Fingers dip at the font, fly
Up to the roof of the forehead
With a sigh.
                    On St. Joseph's
Outstretched arm, he hangs his cap
Then spends a very pleasant mass
Studying the wen-marked heads
Of his neighbours, or gouging
His name in the soft wood
Of the choirloft, with the cross
Of his rosary beads.

In a plain envelope marked: IMPORTANT

THE BREAD GOD

the DEVIL *has* CHRIST *where he wants* HIM
A HELPLESS INFANT IN ARMS: A DEAD CHRIST ON THE CROSS
ROME'S CENTRAL ACT OF WORSHIP IS THE EUCHARISTIC WAFER!
IDOLATRY: THE WORST IDOL UNDER HEAVEN
NOSELESS, EYELESS, EARLESS, HELPLESS, SPEECHLESS.

The crowds for communion, heavy coat and black shawl,
Surge in thick waves, cattle thronged in a fair,
To the oblong of altar rails, and there
Where red berried holly shines against gold
In the door of the tabernacle, wait patient
And prayerful and crowded, for each moment
Of silence, eyes closed, mouth raised
For the advent of the flesh-graced Word.

DEAR BROTHER!
ECUMENISM *is* THE NEW NAME *of the* WHORE OF BABYLON
SHE *who* SHITS *on the* SEVEN HILLS
ONE CHURCH, ONE STATE
WITH THE POPE THE HEAD OF THE STATE: BY RE-UNION
ROME MEANS ABSORPTION
UNIFORMITY MEANS TYRANNY
APISTS = PAPISTS
But GOD DELIGHTS IN VARIETY
NO *two leaves are* EXACTLY *alike!*

Coming out of the chapel
The men were already assembled
Around the oak-tree,
Solid brogues, thick coats.
Staring at the women,
Sheltering cigarettes.

Once a politician came
Climbed on the graveyard wall
And they listened to all
His plans with the same docility;
Eyes quiet, under caps
Like sloped eaves.

Nailed to the wet bark
The notice of a football match;
Pearses *v* Hibernians
Or a Monster Carnival
In aid of Church Funds
Featuring Farrel's Band.

[27]

LOYALISTS REMEMBER!
MILLIONS *have been* MURDERED *for refusing to* GROVEL
Before Rome's Mass-Idol: THE HOST!
King Charles I and his Frog Queen Henrietta GLOAT *in their letters*
that they have almost EXTERMINATED THE PROTESTANTS OF IRELAND
The PRIESTS *in every* PARISH *were told to record* HOW MANY KILLED!
Under ROGER MOORE *and* SIR PHELIM O'NEIL
Instruments of ROME
40,000 loyal protestants were MASSACRED *like game-fowl*
IN ONE NIGHT
Cromwell went to Ireland
TO STOP
The Catholics murdering Protestants!

Penal Rock : Altamuskin

To learn the massrock's lesson, leave your car,
Descend frost gripped steps to where
A humid moss overlaps the valley floor.
Crisp as a pistol-shot, the winter air
Recalls poor Tagues, folding the nap of their frieze
Under one knee, long suffering as beasts,
But parched for that surviving sign of grace,
The bog-latin murmur of their priest.
A crude stone oratory, carved by a cousin,
Commemorates the place. For two hundred years
People of our name have sheltered in this glen
But now all have left. A few flowers
Wither on the altar, so I melt a ball of snow
From the hedge into their rusty tin before I go.

[28]

I sometimes wonder if anyone could have brought the two sides together. Your father, I know, was very bitter about having to leave but when I visited home before leaving for the Australian mission, I found our protestant neighbours friendly, and yet we had lost any position we had in the neighbourhood. You realise of course, that all this has nothing to do with religion; perhaps this new man will find a way to resolve the old hatreds. . . .

An Ulster Prophecy

I saw the Pope breaking stones on Friday,
A blind parson sewing a patchwork quilt,
Two bishops cutting rushes with their croziers,
Roaring Meg firing rosary beads for cannonballs,
Corks in boats afloat on the summit of the Sperrins,
A severed head speaking with a grafted tongue,
A snail paring Royal Avenue with a hatchet,
British troops firing on the Shankill,
A mill and a forge on the back of a cuckoo,
The fox sitting conceitedly at a window chewing tobacco,
And a curlew in flight
                    surveying
                         a United Ireland

IV

A SEVERED HEAD

And who ever heard
Such a sight unsung
As a severed head
With a grafted tongue?
Old Rhyme

To see a souldiour toze a Karne, O Lord it is a wonder!
And eke what care he tak'th to part the head from neck asonder.
John Derricke: *A Discoverie of Woodkarne*, 1581

Sir Thomas Phillips made, a
journey from Coleraine to
Dungannon, through the
wooded country . . . and there-
upon wrote to Salisbury,
expressing . . . his unfeigned
astonishment at the sight of so
many cattle and such abun-
dance of grain. . . . The hill-
sides were literally covered with
cattle . . . the valleys were
clothed in the rich garniture of
ripening barley and oats; while
the woods swarmed with swine
. . . 20,000 of these being easily
fattened yearly in the forest of
Glenconkeyne alone.
George Hill: *An Historical
Account of the Plantation
in Ulster*

Our geographers do not forget
what entertainment the Irish of
Tyrone gave to a mapmaker about
the end of the late great rebellion;
for, one Barkeley being appointed
by the late Earl of Devonshire to
draw a true and perfect map of the
north parts of Ulster . . . when he
came into Tyrone the inhabitants
took off his head. . . .
Sir John Davies

I

May, and the air is light
On eye, on hand. As I take
The mountain road, my former step
Doubles mine, driving cattle
To the upland fields. Between
Shelving ditches of whitethorn
They sway their burdensome
Bodies, tempted at each turn
By hollows of sweet grass,
Pale clover, while memory,
A restive sally switch, flicks
Across their backs.
                    The well
Is still there, a half-way mark
Between two cottages, opposite
The gate in Danaghy's field,
But above the protective dry-
Stone rim, the plaiting thorns
Have not been bill-hooked back
And a thick *glaur* floats.
No need to rush to head off
The cattle from sinking soft
Muzzles into leaf smelling
Spring water.
                    From the farm
Nearby, I hear a yard tap gush
And a collie bark, to check
My presence. Our farmhands
Lived there, wife and children
In twin white-washed cells,
An iron roof burning in summer.
Now there is a kitchen extension
With radio aerial, rough outhouses
For coal and tractor. A housewife
Smiles good-day as I step through
The fluff and dust of her walled
Farmyard, solicited by raw-necked
Stalking turkeys
                    to where cart
Ruts shape the ridge of a valley,

[33]

One of many among the switch-
Back hills of what old chroniclers
Called the Star Bog. Croziered
Fern, white scut of *ceannbhán*,
Spars of bleached bog fir jutting
From heather, make a landscape
So light in wash it must be learnt
Day after day, in shifting detail,
Out to the pale Sperrins.
'I like to look across,' said
Barney Horisk leaning on his *sleán*
'and think of all the people
Who have bin.'
                    Like shards
Of a lost culture, the slopes
Are strewn with cabins, deserted
In my lifetime. Here the older
People sheltered; the Blind Nialls,
Big Ellen, who had been a Fair-
Day prostitute. The bushes cramp
To the evening wind as I reach
The road's end. Jamie MacCrystal
Lived in the final cottage,
A trim grove of mountain ash
Soughed protection round his walls
And bright painted gate. The thatch
Has slumped in, white dust of nettles
On the flags. Only the shed remains
In use for calves, although fuschia
Bleeds by the wall, and someone has
Propped a yellow cartwheel
Against the door.

2

All around, shards of a lost tradition:
From the Rough Field I went to school
In the Glen of the Hazels. Close by
Was the bishopric of the Golden Stone;
The cairn of Carleton's homesick poem.

Scattered over the hills, tribal
And placenames, uncultivated pearls.

[34]

No rock or ruin, dun or dolmen
But showed memory defying cruelty
Through an image-encrusted name.

The heathery gap where the Rapparee,
Shane Barnagh, saw his brother die —
On a summer's day the dying sun
Stained its colours to crimson:
So breaks the heart, Brish-mo-Cree.

The whole landscape a manuscript
We had lost the skill to read,
A part of our past disinherited;
But fumbled, like a blind man,
Along the fingertips of instinct.

The last Gaelic speaker in the parish
When I stammered my school Irish
One Sunday after mass, crinkled
A rusty litany of praise:
Tá an Ghaeilge againn arís . . .

Tír Eoghain: Land of Owen,
Province of the O'Niall;
The ghostly tread of O'Hagan's
Barefoot gallowglasses marching
To merge forces in Dun Geanainn

Push southward to Kinsale!
Loudly the war-cry is swallowed
In swirls of black rain and fog
As Ulster's pride, Elizabeth's foemen,
Founder in a Munster bog.

3

'O'Neill: A name more in price
than to be called Caesar.'
Sir George Carew

Con Bacach O'Neill, 1542

Heralded by trumpeters,
Prefaced by a bishop,
Sided by earls, Con
The lame limps down
The palace at Greenwich.

[35]

Twenty angels for
A fur lined gown,
Ten white pounds
To the College of Arms
For a new escutcheon
That he may kneel on
The deep strewn rushes
To hear Henry's command;
When the bugles sound —
Forty shillings, by custom,
Must go to the captain —
His knee lifts rustily
From English ground:
Arise, Earl of Tyrone.

Seán an Diomas, 1562

Swarthy and savage as
The dream of a conquistador,
Seán O'Niall, Shane
The Proud struts before
The first Elizabeth.
Her fine-hosed courtiers
Stare at his escort
Of tall gallowglasses,
Long hair curling
Over saffron shirts
With, on each shoulder —
Under the tangle of
The forbidden glib —
The dark death-sheen
Of the battle axe.

Hugh, 1599

Around the table
Of the Great O'Neill
(Crushed bracken or
A stone slab, under
A cloudless heaven)
Sir John Harington sees
The princely children
In velvet jerkin

[36]

And gold lace, after
The English fashion
With a bodyguard of
Beardless, half-naked
Boys, all listening
Meek as spaniels
While, with the aid
Of the shy poet tutor
He reads his translation
Of Ariosto's canto
On Fortune's Wheel
Whither 'runs a
Restless round.'

After Kinsale, 1604

A messenger from the Pale
Found the hunted rebel
Living, like a wood kerne,
In the wet meadows near
His broken coronation stone.
From Tullyhogue
He rides to Mellifont
To kneel for an hour
Before the Lord Deputy
'Most sorrowfully imploring'
Her Sacred Majesty,
Promising to abjure
'All barbarous custom'
His tribal title, O'Neill.
Mountjoy embraces him
Omitting to mention
That the red-haired queen
He so reverently entreats
Is dead a week.

[37]

4

This was a distinguished crew for one
ship; for it is indeed certain that the
sea had not supported, and the winds
had not wafted from Ireland, in
modern times, a party of one ship
who would have been more illustrious,
or noble in point of genealogy, or
more renowned for deeds, valour or
high achievements. . . .
Annals of the Four Masters

> The fiddler settles in
> to his playing so easily;
> rosewood box tucked under chin,
> saw of rosined bow
> & angle of elbow
>
> that the mind elides
> for a while what he plays:
> hornpipe or reel to warm
> us up well, heel or toecap
> twitching in tune
>
> till the sound expands
> in the slow climb of a lament.
> As by some forest campfire
> listeners draw near, to honour
> a communal loss
>
> & a shattered procession
> of anonymous suffering
> files through the brain:
> burnt houses, pillaged farms,
> a province in flames.

We have killed, burnt and despoiled
all along the Lough to within four
miles of Dungannon . . . in which
journeys we have killed above a
hundred of all sorts, besides such as
we have burned, how many I know
not. We spare none, of what quality or
sex soever, and it had bred much
terror in the people who heard not a
drum nor saw not a fire of long time.
Chichester to Mountjoy, Spring 1607

With an intricate
& mournful mastery
the thin bow glides & slides,
assuaging like a bardic poem,
our tribal pain —

Disappearance & death
of a world, as down Lough Swilly
the great ship, encumbered with nobles,
swells its sails for Europe:
The Flight of the Earls.

5

(Dumb,
bloodied, the severed
head now chokes to
speak another tongue —

As in
a long suppressed dream,
some stuttering garb-
led ordeal of my own.)

An Irish
child weeps at school
repeating its English.
After each mistake

The master
gouges another mark
on the tally stick
hung about its neck

Like a bell
on a cow, a hobble
on a straying goat.
To slur and stumble

In shame
the altered syllables
of your own name;
to stray sadly home

And find
the turf cured width
of your parent's hearth
growing slowly alien:

In cabin
and field, they still
speak the old tongue.
You may greet no one.

To grow
a second tongue, as
harsh a humiliation
as twice to be born.

Decades later
that child's grandchild's
speech stumbles over lost
syllables of an old order.

6

Yet even English in these airts
Took a lawless turn, as who
Would not stroll by Bloody Brae
To Black Lough, or guddle trout
In a stream called the Routing Burn?

Or rest a while on Crooked Bridge
Up the path to Crow Hill;
Straight by Ania's Cove to Spur Royal,
Then round by Duck Island
To Green Mount and New Town Civil?

A last look over the dark ravine
Where that red-tufted rebel,
The Todd, out-leaped the pack;
Turning home by Favour Royal
And the forests of Dourless Black.

And what of stone-age Sess Kill Green
Tullycorker and Tullyglush?
Names twining braid Scots and Irish,
Like Fall Brae, springing native
As a whitethorn bush?

A high, stony place — bogstreams,
Not milk and honey — but our own:
From the Glen of the Hazels
To the Golden Stone may be
The longest journey
      I have ever gone.

V

THE FAULT

I hope Lynch will not be
executed for I know he knew
nothing of this till the last
moment, though at the last
meeting of the Council he
consented by his silence when
I alone opposed it. I was told
Tyrone was not Ireland, and
that I could not take a correct
view of the situation from the
position of Tyrone.
Dr. Patrick McCartan
May 1916

Then came the Great War....
Great empires have been over-
turned. . . . The position of
countries has been violently
altered. The modes of thought
of men, the whole outlook on
affairs, the grouping of parties,
all have encountered tremen-
dous changes. . . . But as the
deluge subsides and the waters
fall short we see the dreary
steeples of Fermanagh and
Tyrone emerging once again.
The integrity of their quarrel
is one of the few institutions
that has been unaltered by the
cataclysm.
Winston Churchill 1922

I

Stele for a Northern Republican

Once again, with creased forehead
and trembling hands, my father calls
me from stifling darkness. . . .
Little enough I know of your struggle,
although you come to me more and more,
free of that heavy body armour
you tried to dissolve with alcohol,
a pale face straining in dream light
like a fish's belly
                        upward to life.
Hesitantly, I trace your part in
the holy war to restore our country,

[42]

slipping from home to smoke
an absentee's mansion, concoct
ambushes. Games turned serious
when the cross-fire at Falban
riddled the tender of policemen,
one bleeding badly
                              stretched upon
the stone flags of our kitchen,
your sisters moving in a whisper
of blood and bandages. Strange war
when the patrol scouted bales
of fodder, stray timber, tar
to prepare those sheltering walls
for reprisal's savage flames
if he should die!
                         That night
you booked into a Strabane hotel.
'Locals were rarely used for jobs:
orders of the Dublin organizer,
shot afterwards, by his own side.'
A generation later, the only sign
of your parochial struggle was
when the plough rooted rusty guns,
dull bayonets, in some rushy glen
for us to play with.
                            Although again
and again, the dregs of disillusion
churned in our Northern parents' guts
to set their children's teeth on edge;
my mother hobbling to the shed
to burn the Free State uniforms
her two brothers had thrown off
(frugal, she saved the buttons):
my father, home from the boat at Cobh,
staring in pale anger at a Redmond
Commemoration stamp
                            or tearing to
flitters the polite Masscard sent
by a Catholic policeman. But what if
you have no country to set before Christ,
only a broken province? No parades,
fierce medals, will mark Tyrone's re-birth,

[43]

betrayed by both South and North;
so lie still, difficult old man,
you were right to choose a Brooklyn slum
rather than a half-life in this
by-passed and dying place.

2

Fault

When I am angry, sick or tired
A line on my forehead pulses,
The line on my left temple
Opened by an old car accident.
My father had the same scar
In the same place, as if
The same fault ran through
Us both: anger, impatience,
A stress born of violence.

3

Sound of a Wound

    Who knows
the sound a wound makes?
    Scar tissue
can rend, the old hurt
    tear open as
the torso of the fiddle
    groans to
carry the tune, to carry
    the pain of
a lost (slow herds of cattle
    roving over
soft meadow, dark bogland)
    pastoral rhythm.

[44]

I assert
a civilisation died here;
        it trembles
underfoot where I walk these
        small, sad hills:
it rears in my blood stream
        when I hear
a bleat of Saxon condescension,
        Westminster
to hell, it is less than these
        strangely carved
five thousand year resisting stones,
        that lonely cross.

        This bitterness
I inherit from my father, the
        swarm of blood
to the brain, the vomit surge
        of race hatred,
the victim seeing the oppressor,
        bold Jacobean
planter, or gadget laden marine,
        who has scatter-
ed his household gods, used
        his people
as servants, flushed his women
        like game.

4

Cage

My father, the least happy
man I have known. His face
retained the pallor
of those who work underground:
the lost years in Brooklyn
listening to a subway
shudder the earth.

But a traditional Irishman
who (released from his grille
in the Clark Street I.R.T.)
drank neat whiskey until
he reached the only element
he felt at home in
any longer: brute oblivion.

And yet picked himself
up, most mornings,
to march down the street
extending his smile
to all sides of the good,
(all-white) neighbourhood
belled by St Teresa's church.

When he came back
we walked together
across fields of Garvaghey
to see hawthorn on the summer
hedges, as though
he had never left;
a bend of the road

which still sheltered
primroses. But we
did not smile in
the shared complicity
of a dream, for when
weary Odysseus returns
Telemachus should leave.

Often as I descend
into subway or underground
I see his bald head behind
the bars of the small booth;
the mark of an old car
accident beating on his
ghostly forehead.

VI

A GOOD NIGHT

The inhabitants of the region
are as impenetrable as rocks. . . .
You talk to them, and in the
depth of their eyes it can be
seen that they don't believe.
Che Guevera

It was the whiskey in his head
No harm was in his mind
He happened for to tell too loud
The way his thoughts inclined.
Old Rhyme

As I was going
Through a guttery gap
I met me Uncle Davy:
I cut his throat
And drank his blood
And left his body aisy.
Old Riddle

I

Up for Sale

> We meet that evening in The Last Sheaf
> Which has gained mocking notoriety
> Since the boss began to diminish
> His own stock. A distempered house
> At a crossroads, we mount guard
> On neighbours cycling heavily past
> As we jostle at the deal bar
> In a brackish stour of stout,
> Paraffin, stale bread.
>   After hours
> All hands shift to the kitchen,
> Snap down the blinds! Our light
> Is a grease fattened candle, but
> In our gloomy midnight cave
> No one minds, we have reached
> The singing stage. 'The Orange Flute',
> 'The Mountains of Pomeroy', the songs
> That survive in this sparse soil
> Are quavered out, until someone
> Remembers to call on Packy Farrel
> *To say a song.*
>   With the almost
> Professional shyness of the folk-singer
> He keeps us waiting, until he rises,
> Head forced back, eyeballs blind.

An Bunnán Buí. As the Gaelic
Rises and recedes, swirling deep
To fall back, all are silent,
Tentacles of race seeking to sound
That rough sadness. At the climax
He grips the chair before him
Until the knuckles whiten —
Sits down abruptly as he rose.
Man looks at man, the current
Of community revived to a near-
ly perfect round . . .
                              Soon broken
As talks expands, in drunken detail.
'I said to him': 'He swore to me.'
With smart alec roughness, Henry
Rakes up our family history:
'Was it patriotism, or bankruptcy?'
Austin Donnelly remembers our fight
Over a swallow's nest, a caning
For peering under the Girls' Lavatory.
An owl-sad child, shaken from sleep,
Watches us, in a tatty night-shirt.
'A crying shame,' sighs one, but his
Publican father is so far gone, he
No longer bothers to trek to the bar
But strikes bottles on the flange
Of the Raeburn, until the floor
Is littered with green splinters
Of glass, tintops.
                        It is the usual
Grotesque, half animal evening so
Common in Ireland, with much glum
Contrariness, much disappearing
Into the darkness, before we group
Outside, trying to mutter *Goodnight.*
My companions now feel the need
To continue. Fit as fiddles,
Fresh as daisies, we plan the next move;
The moon on the road is a river
Of light, leading to new adventure . . .

[49]

The Fight

When I found the swallow's
Nest under the bridge —
Ankle deep in the bog stream,
Traffic drumming overhead —
I was so pleased, I ran
To fetch a school companion
To share the nude fragility
Of the shells, lightly freckled
With colour, in their cradle
Of feathers, twigs, earth.

It was still breast warm
Where I curved in my hand
To count them, one by one
Into his cold palm, a kind
Of trophy or offering. Turn-
Ing my back, to scoop out
The last, I heard him run
Down the echoing hollow
Of the bridge. Splashing
After, I bent tangled in
Bull wire at the bridge's
Mouth, when I saw him take
And break them, one by one
Against a sunlit stone.

For minutes we fought
Standing and falling in
The river's brown spate,
And I would still fight
Though now I can forgive.

To worship or destroy beauty —
That double edge of impulse
I recognise, by which we live;
But also the bitter paradox
Of betraying love to harm,
Then lungeing, too late,
With fists, to its defence.

3

Three things to startle that day:
The flat, helpless way Henry's milk
Horse fell, as we raced to school,
And how, as we tiptoed in late,
The damp coats of the scholars
Stood breathing in the hall.
Last, at lunchtime, as the boys
Scuffled a string and paper ball
Over the gravel, a white Catalina
From the Erne base (an old pupil)
Rose out of a hole in the hedge,
Sudden as a flying swan, to circle
Over the school in salutation
And fold into cloud again.

4

Plan the next move. *Whereabouts?*
Don't forget the case of stout.
Which only means that, dragging
A crate of bottles between us,
A rump parliament of old friends
Spend the lees of the night in
A mountain cottage, swapping
Stories, till cock-crow warns
Then stagger home, drunk as coots,
Through the sleeping countryside.

A gate clangs, I grope against
A tent-fold of darkness until
Eye accepts the animal shape
Of the hedge, the sphere of
Speckled sky, the pale, damp
Fields breathing on either side.
The lane is smoothly tarred
Downhill to the humped bridge
Where I peer uncertainly over,

[51]

Lured towards sense by the
Unseen rattle of this mountain
Stream, whose lowland idlings
Define my townland's shape.

I climbed to its source once,
A journey perilous, through
The lifeless, lichened thorn
Of MacCrystal's Glen, a thread
Of water still leading me on
Past stale bog-cuttings, gray
Shapes slumped in rusty bracken,
Littered with fir's white bone:
Stranded mammoths! The water's
Thin music unwinding upwards
Till, high on a ledge of pale
Reeds and heather, I came
Upon a pool of ebony water
Fenced by rocks . . .
                                    Legend
Declared a monster trout
Lived there, so I slipped
A hand under the fringe of
Each slick rock, splitting
The skin of turning froth
To find nothing but that
Wavering pulse leading to
The central heart where
The spring beat, so icy-cold
I shiver now in recollection,
Hearing its brisk, tireless
Movement over the pebbles
Beneath my feet . . .
                                    Was that
The ancient trout of wisdom
I meant to catch? As I plod
Through the paling darkness
Details emerge, and memory
Warms. Old Danaghy raging
With his stick, to keep our
Cows from a well, that now
Is boarded up, like himself.

[52]

Here his son and I robbed a
Bee's nest, kicking the combs
Free; our boots smelt sweetly
For days afterwards. Snowdrop
In March, primrose in April,
Whitethorn in May, cardinal's
Fingers of foxglove dangling
All summer: every crevice held
A secret sweetness. Remembering,
I seem to smell wild honey
On my face.
            And plunge
Down the hillside, singing
In a mood of fierce elation.
My seven league boots devour
Time and space as I crash
Through the last pools of
Darkness. All around, my
Neighbours sleep, but I am
In possession of their past
(The pattern history weaves
From one small backward place)
Marching through memory magnified:
Each grassblade bends with
Translucent beads of moisture
And the bird of total meaning
Stirs upon its hidden branch.
As I reach the last lap
The seventh sense of drunkenness —
That extra pilot in the head —
Tells me I am being watched
And wheeling, I confront a clump
Of bullocks. Inert in grass,
They gaze at me, saucer-eyed,
Turning their slow surprise
Upon their tongue. *Store cattle*:
The abattoirs of old England
Will soon put paid to them. In
A far meadow, the corncrake
Turns its rusty ratchet and
I find myself rounding the
Last corner towards the black
Liquid gleam of the main road.

[53]

In five years, showbands have
become the most important
part of the Irish entertainment
industry. About 10,000 ball-
rooms, small halls, clubs giving
full or part-time employment
to about 100,000 people, while
between six and seven thousand
musicians play with 700
professional and semi-
professional bands.

5

Dancehall

And there, on a ravaged hillock
    overlooking the road,
the raw inheritor of this place,
    an unfinished hall.
Stung to soberness in the dawn
    I sway and stare.
Its blank eyes — gaps in concrete —
    stare blindly back.

Seemsh no escape. Poet and object
    must conshumate.
No lyric memory softens the fact —
    this stone idol
could house more hopes than any
    verse of mine.
I eye its girdered skeleton
    with brute respect.

Three miles away, a gutted castle
    stands; Sir John's
which my father helped to burn.
    Its elegant remains
still dominate the district, as
    now this Roseland
shall, a concrete prow cargoed
    with vague dreams.

[54]

The shiny roofs of cars, shoals
    of minnows, may
swim around it, pairs stumble from
    the wide light
of the door to the narrow privacy
    of plastic seats.
A sigh, a kiss, hands wander
    near thin skirts

as music shakes & pounds.
    An industry built
on loneliness, setting the young
    to clamber over
each other, brief as mayflies
    in their hunger
for novelty, for flashing
    energy & change . . .

Both *Barde* and Harper is preparde, which by their cunning art,
Doe strike and cheare up all the gestes with comfort at the hart.
John Derricke, 1581.

[55]

VII

HYMN TO
THE NEW OMAGH ROAD

As the bull-dozer bites into the tree ringed hillfort
Its grapnel jaws lift the mouse, the flower,
With equal attention, and the plaited twigs
And clay of the bird's nest, shaken by the traffic,
Fall from a crevice under the bridge
Into the slow-flowing mud choked stream
Below the quarry, where the mountain trout
Turns up its pale belly to die.

Balance Sheet

𝕷𝖔𝖘𝖘

Item: The shearing away of an old barn
criss-cross of beams where pigeons moan
high small window where the swallow built
white-washed dry-stone walls

Item: The suppression of stone lined paths
old potato-boiler full of crocuses
overhanging lilac or laburnum
sweet pea climbing the fence.

Item: The filling-in of chance streams
uncovered wells, all unchannelled sources
of water that might weaken foundations
bubbling over the macadam.

Item: The disappearance of all signs
of wild life, wren's or robin's nest,
a rabbit nibbling a coltsfoot leaf,
a stray squirrel or water rat.

Item: The uprooting of wayside hedges
with their accomplices, devil's bit and pee the bed,
prim rose and dog rose, an unlawful
assembly of thistles.

Item: The removal of all hillocks
and humps, superstition styled fairy forts
and long barrows, now legally to be regarded
as obstacles masking a driver's view.

[58]

Gain

Item: 10 men from the district being for a period of time
fully employed, their ten wives could buy groceries
and clothes to send 30 children content to school for a
few months, and raise local merchants' hearts by
paying their bills.

Item: A man driving from Belfast to Londonderry can
arrive a quarter of an hour earlier, a lorry load of
goods ditto, thus making Ulster more competitive
in the international market.

Item: A local travelling from the prefabricated suburbs of
bypassed villages can manage an average of 50
rather than 40 m.p.h. on his way to see relatives in
Omagh hospital or lunatic asylum.

Item: The dead of Garvaghey Graveyard (including my
grandfather) can have an unobstructed view—the trees
having been sheared away for a carpark — of the living
passing at great speed, sometimes quick enough to
come straight in:

Let it be clear
That I do not grudge my grandfather
This long delayed pleasure!
I like the idea of him
Rising from the rotting boards of the coffin
With his J.P.'s white beard
And penalising drivers
For travelling faster
Than jaunting cars

[59]

2

From the quarry behind the school
the crustacean claws of the excavator
rummage to withdraw a payload,
a giant's bite . . .

'Tis pleasant for to take a stroll by Glencull Waterside
On a lovely evening in spring (in nature's early pride);
You pass by many a flowery bank and many a shady dell,
Like walking through enchanted land where fairies used to dwell

Tuberous tentacles
of oak, hawthorn, buried pignut,
the topsoil of a living shape
of earth lifts like a scalp
to lay open

The trout are rising to the fly; the lambkins sport and play;
The pretty feathered warblers are singing by the way;
The black birds' and the thrushes' notes, by the echoes multiplied,
Do fill the vale with melody by Glencull waterside.

slipping sand
shale, compressed veins of rock,
old foundations, a soft chaos
to be swallowed wholesale,
masticated, regurgitated
by the mixer.

Give not to me the rugged scenes of which some love to write —
The beetling cliffs, o'erhanging crags and the eagle in full flight
But give to me the fertile fields (the farmer's joy and pride)
The homestead and the orchards fine by Glencull waterside.

Secret places
birds' nests, animal paths,
ghosts of children hunkering
down snail glistering slopes
spin through iron cylinders to
resume new life as a pliant stream
of building material.

These scenes bring recollections back to comrades scattered wide
Who used with me to walk these banks in youthful manly pride;
They've left their boyhood's happy homes and crossed o'er oceans wide
Now but in dreamland may they walk by Glencull waterside.

A brown stain
seeps away from where the machine
rocks and groans to itself, dis-
colouring the grass, thickening
the current of the trout stream
which flows between broken banks
— the Waterside a smear of mud —
towards the reinforced bridge
of the new road.

3

My sympathy goes out to the farmer
who, mad drunk after a cattle mart,
bought himself a concrete swan
for thirty bob, and lugged it
all the way
home
to deposit it
(where the monkey puzzle was meant to grow)
on his tiny landscaped lawn.

VIII

PATRIOTIC SUITE

FOR SEAN O RIADA

They say it is the Fatal Destiny
of that land that no purposes
whatsoever which are meant for
her good will prosper.
Edmund Spenser

The real aims of a revolution.
those which are not illusions,
are always to be realised after
that revolution.
Engels

I

Again that note! A weaving
melancholy, like a bird crossing
moorland;
           pale ice on a corrie
opening inward, soundless harp-
strings of rain:
              the pathos
of last letters in the 1916 Room,
'Mother, I thank . . .'
                a podgy landmine,
Pearse's swordstick leading to a care-
fully profiled picture.
                 That point
where folk and art meet, murmurs
Herr Doktor as
              the wail of tin
whistle climbs against fiddle and
the *bodhrán* begins —
                  lost cry
of the yellow bittern!

2

The mythic lyre shrunk to country size:
The clatter of brogues on the flagstones,
The colourless dram of poteen —
Is that the world we were made for?

3

Smell of appleblossom in the air,
Step of a huntress on the stair.

In Bedford Park a young man waits
Still warm at the heart of family
But fearful what life, the hazard
Of his slight gift, holds in store:

'I was about to learn that the poet
Must be shaped by luckless luck
Into saint, lover or philosopher.'

Smell of appleblossom in the air,
Step of a goddess on the stair.

4

Symbolic depth-charge of music
Releases a national dream;
From clerk to paladin
In a single violent day.
Files of men from shattered buildings
(Slouch hat, blunt mauser gun)
Frame the freedom that they won.

The bread queue, the messianic
Agitator of legend
Arriving on the train —
Christ and socialism —
Wheatfield and factory
Vivid in the sun:
Connolly's dream, if any one.

All revolutions are interior
The displacement of spirit
By the arrival of fact,
Ceaseless as cloud across sky,
Sudden as sun.
Movement of a butterfly
Modifies everything.

[65]

5

The tribes merged into the hills,
The ultimate rocks where seals converse.
There they supped rain-water, ate sparse
Berries and (grouped around pale fires
At evening) comforted themselves
With runics of verse.

The nation forgot them until
There was a revolution. Then soldiers
Clambered the slopes, saluting
In friendliness: 'Come down!
You are the last pride of our race,
Herdsmen aristocrats, who have kept the faith.'

As they strayed through the vertical cities
Everyone admired their blue eyes, open smiles
(Vowels, like flowers, caught in the teeth)
The nervous majesty of their gait:
To the boredom of pavements they brought
The forgotten grace of the beast.

Soon townspeople tired of them,
Begin to deride their smell, their speech.
Some returned. Others stayed behind,
Accommodating themselves to a new language.
In either case, they may be dying out.
A tragedy anticipated in the next government report.

6

Enterprise

The train crawls across a bridge:
Through the cantilevered interstices
— A lace curtain monstrously magnified —
We overlook the sprawling town.

Row after row of council cottages
Ride the hill, curving up to the church
Or down to the docks
Where a crane tilts into emptiness.

[66]

Here nothing has been planned —
Assembled, yes, casual
And coarse as detritus,
Affronting eye and mind.

Only a drift of smoke
And the antlike activity of cars
Indicate life; with the wild flap
Of laundry in a thousand backyards.

Soon we are running through summer fields
Where a roller is at work
Bruising neat stripes of corn
Under hawthorn hedges, patterned in white flame.

7

Take Your Stand

The visitor to Coole Park
in search of a tradition
finds
     a tangled alley-way
a hint of foundation wall
(the kitchen floor)
          high wire
to protect the famous beech-tree
from raw initials
       and a lake
bereft of swans.

Stable

Before the film the censor's script
Flashes on the screen.
I hardly notice it
So deeply has the
Harness worn in.

Build-Up

Elegant port-wine brick, a colonial dream:
Now we own the cow, why keep the cream?

[67]

8

During 1960/1 the Irish attained
many high positions abroad and
the national economy, for the first
time in history, showed an upward
trend. Only the Vatican continued
to ignore us.

World-witnessed, our spiritual empire
After years so long enduring
That suffering became a form of speech
With all our songs plangent or soft:
Does fate at last relent
With a trade expansion of 5 per cent?

Now the unsmiling Saxon, surprised
And diffident, greets an equal
As, exemplary in the Congo,
Rational in the U.N.,
We prospect the lands beyond
Kipling's setting sun.

Already a shocked Belfast beholds
A black veiled Queen enter the Vatican.
Through Washington and Canterbury
All roads lead to Rome.
Granted a saint, we might shepherd
Another Dark Ages home.

9

At the Fleadh Cheoil in Mullingar
There were two sounds, the breaking
Of glass, and the background pulse
Of music. Young girls roamed
The streets with eager faces,
Shoving for men. Bottles in
Hand, they rowed out for a song:
Puritan Ireland's dead and gone,
A myth of O'Connor and O Faoláin.

[68]

In the early morning the lovers
Lay on both sides of the canal
Listening on Sony transistors
To the agony of Pope John.
Yet it didn't seem strange or blasphemous,
This ground bass of death and
Resurrection, as we strolled along:
Puritan Ireland's dead and gone,
A myth of O'Connor and O Faoláin.

Further on, breasting the wind
Waves of the deserted grain harbour
We saw a pair, a cob and his pen,
Most nobly linked. Everything then
In our casual morning vision
Seemed to flow in one direction,
Line simple as a song:
Puritan Ireland's dead and gone,
A myth of O'Connor and O Faoláin.

I O

The gloomy images of a provincial catholicism

(in a thousand schoolrooms
children work quietly while
Christ bleeds on the wall)

wound in a native music
curlew echoing tin whistle
to eye-swimming melancholy

is that our offering?

While all Europe seeks
new versions of old ways,
the hammer of Boulez swing-
ing to Eastern harmonies.

From 1960 the Gross National Product . . .

Sight of the Skelligs at sunset
restores our Hy-Brasil:
the Atlantic expands on the cliffs
the herring gull claims the air

again that note!

                  above a self-drive car.

IX

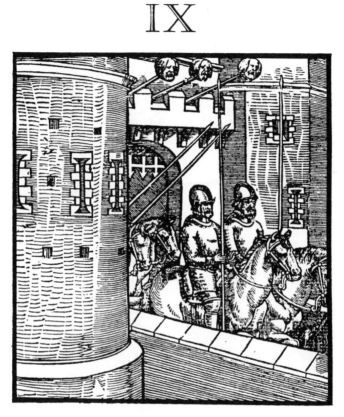

A NEW SIEGE

FOR BERNADETTE DEVLIN

Once again, it happens.
Under a barrage of stones
and flaring petrol bombs
the blunt, squat shape of
an armoured car glides
into the narrow streets
of the Catholic quarter
leading a file of helmet-
ed, shielded riot police;
once again, it happens,
like an old Troubles film,
run for the last time . . .

Lines of history
   lines of power
the long sweep
   of the Bogside
under the walls
   up to Creggan
the black muzzle
   of Roaring Meg
staring dead on
   cramped houses
the jackal shapes
   of James's army
watching the city
   stiffen in siege

Lines of defiance
   lines of discord
near the Diamond
   brisk with guns
British soldiers
   patrol the walls
the gates between
   Ulster Catholic
Ulster Protestant
   a Saracen slides
past the Guildhall
   a black Cuchulain
bellowing against
   the Scarlet Whore
twin races petrified
   the volcanic ash
of religious hatred

SMALL SHOT HATH
   POURED LIKE HAIL
THE GREAT GUNS
   SHAKEN OUR WALLS
a spectral garrison
   no children left
sick from eating
   horseflesh, vermin
curs fattened on
   the slain Irish
still flaunting
   the bloody flag
of 'No Surrender'
   GOD HAS MADE US
AN IRON PILLAR
   AND BRAZEN WALLS
AGAINST THIS LAND.

symbol of Ulster
   these sloping streets
blackened walls
   sick at heart and
seeking a sign
   the flaghung gloom
of St. Columb's
   the brass eagle of
the lectern bearing
   the Sermon on the Mount
in its shoulders
   'A city that is
set on a hill
   cannot be hid.'

Columba's Derry!
  ledge of angels
radiant oakwood
  where the man dove
knelt to master
  his fiery temper
exile chastened
  the bright candle
of the Uí Néill
  burns from Iona
lightens Scotland
  with beehive huts
glittering manuscripts
  but he remembers
his secret name
  'He who set his
back on Ireland.'

Rearing westward
  the great sunroom
of Inis Eoghain
  coiling stones of
Aileach's hillfort
  higher than Tara
the Hy Niall
  dominating Uladh
the white cone
  of Sliabh Snacht
sorrow veiled
  the silent fjord
is uaigneach Eire
  as history's wind
plucks a dynasty
  from the ramparts
bids a rival
  settlement rise

Lines of leaving
  lines of returning
the long estuary
  of Lough Foyle, a
ship motionless
  in wet darkness
mournfully hooting
  as a tender creeps
to carry passengers
  back to Ireland
a child of four
  this sad sea city
my landing place
  the loneliness of
Lir's white daughter's
  ice crusted wings
forever spread
  at the harbour mouth.

London's Derry!
  METHOUGHT I SAW
DIDOE'S COLONY
  BUILDING OF CARTHAGE
culverin and saker
  line strong walls
but local chiefs
  come raging in
O'Cahan, O'Doherty
  (a Ferrara sword
his visiting card)
  a New Plantation
a new mythology
  Lundy slides
down a peartree
  as drum and fife
trill ORANJE BOVEN!

Lines of suffering
  lines of defeat
under the walls
  ghetto terraces
sharp pallor of
  unemployed shades
slope shouldered
  broken bottles
pubs and bookies
  red brick walls
Falls or Shankill
  Lecky or Fountain
love's alleyway
  message scrawled
Popehead: Tague
  my own name
hatred's synonym

Lines of protest
  lines of change
a drum beating
  across Berkeley
all that Spring
  invoking the new
Christ avatar
  of the Americas
running voices
  streets of Berlin
Paris, Chicago
  seismic waves
zigzagging through
  a faulty world

But will the meek
inherit the earth?
RELIGION POISONS US
NORTH AND SOUTH.
  A SPECIAL FORCE OF
ANGELS WE'D NEED
  TO PUT MANNERS ON US.
IF THE YOUNG WERE
  HONEST, THEY'D ADMIT
THEY DON'T HOLD
  WITH THE HALF OF IT.
THE SHOWBANDS
  AND THE BORDER HALLS
THAT'S THE STUFF
  Said the guardian
of the empty church
  pale siege windows
shining behind us

Overflowing from
  narrow streets
cramped fields
  a pressure rising
to match it
  tired marchers
nearing Burntollet
  young arms linked
banners poled high
  the baptism of
flying missiles
  spiked clubs
Law and Order's
  medieval armour
of glass shield
  and dangling baton

[74]

Lines of action
  lines of reaction
the white elephant
  of Stormont, Carson's
raised right claw
  a Protestant parliament
a Protestant people
  major this and
captain that and
  general nothing
the bland, pleasant
  face of mediocrity
confronting in horror
  its mirror image
bull-voiced bigotry

Lines of loss
  lines of energy
always changing
  always returning
A TIDE LIFTS
  THE RELIEF SHIP
OFF THE MUD
  OVER THE BOOM
the rough field
  of the universe
growing, changing
  a net of energies
crossing patterns
  weaving towards
a new order
  a new anarchy
always different
  always the same

the emerging order
  of the poem invaded
by cries, protestations
  a people's pain
the defiant face
  of a young girl
campaigning against
  memory's mortmain
a blue banner
  lifting over a
broken province
  DRIVE YOUR PLOUGH
a yellow bulldozer
  raising the rubble
a humming factory
  a housing estate
hatreds sealed into
  a hygienic honeycomb

Across the border
  a dead man
drives to school
  past the fort
at Greene Castle
  a fury of love
for North, South
  eats his heart
on the far side
  a rocky promontory
his family name
  O'Cahan, O'Kane
my uncle watches
  sails upon Foyle
(a flock of swans)
  drives forward

X

THE WILD DOG ROSE

I

I go to say goodbye to the *cailleach*
that terrible figure who haunted my childhood
but no longer harsh, a human being
merely, hurt by event.

          The cottage,
circled by trees, weathered to admonitory
shapes of desolation by the mountain winds,
straggles into view. The rank thistles
and leathery bracken of untilled fields
stretch behind with — a final outcrop —
the hooped figure by the roadside,
its retinue of dogs

          which gave tongue
as I approach, with savage, whining cries
so that she slowly turns, a moving nest
of shawls and rags, to view, to stare
the stranger down.

          And I feel again
that ancient awe, the terror of a child
before the great hooked nose, the cheeks
dewlapped with dirt, the staring blue
of the sunken eyes, the mottled claws
clutching a stick

          but now hold
and return her gaze, to greet her,
as she greets me, in friendliness.
Memories have wrought reconciliation
between us, we talk in ease at last,
like old friends, lovers almost,
sharing secrets

          of neighbours
she quarrelled with, who now lie
in Garvaghey graveyard, beyond all hatred;
of my family and hers, how she never married,
though a man came asking in her youth

[78]

'You would be loath to leave your own,'
she sighs, 'and go among strangers' —
his parish ten miles off.

                         For sixty years
since she has lived alone, in one place.
Obscurely honoured by such confidences,
I idle by the summer roadside, listening,
while the monologue falters, continues,
rehearsing the small events of her life.
The only true madness is loneliness,
the monotonous voice in the skull
that never stops
                    because never heard.

                    2

And there
where the dog rose shines in the hedge
she tells me a story so terrible
that I try to push it away,
my bones melting.

                    Late at night
a drunk came beating at her door
to break it in, the bolt snapping
from the soft wood, the thin mongrels
rushing to cut, but yelping as
he whirls with his farm boots
to crush their skulls.

                    In the darkness
they wrestle, two creatures crazed
with loneliness, the smell of the
decaying cottage in his nostrils
like a drug, his body heavy on hers,
the tasteless trunk of a seventy year
old virgin, which he rummages while
she battles for life

[79]

                    bony fingers
reaching desperately to push
against his bull neck. 'I prayed
to the Blessed Virgin herself
for help and after a time
I broke his grip.'

                    He rolls
to the floor, snores asleep,
while she cowers until dawn
and the dogs' whimpering starts
him awake, to lurch back across
the wet bog.

3

                    And still
the dog rose shines in the hedge.
Petals beaten wide by rain, it
sways slightly, at the tip of a
slender, tangled, arching branch
which, with her stick, she gathers
into us.

                    'The wild rose
is the only rose without thorns,'
she says, holding a wet blossom
for a second, in a hand knotted
as the knob of her stick.
'Whenever I see it, I remember
the Holy Mother of God and
all she suffered.'

                    Briefly
the air is strong with the smell
of that weak flower, offering
its crumbled yellow cup
and pale bleeding lips
fading to white

                    at the rim
of each bruised and heart-
shaped petal.

EPILOGUE

Driving South, we pass through Cavan,
lakeside orchards in first bloom,
hawthorn with a surplice whiteness,
binding the small holdings of Monaghan.

A changing rural pattern means clack
of tractor for horse, sentinel shape
of silo, hum of milking machine:
the same from Ulster to the Ukraine.

Only a sentimentalist would wish
to see such degradation again:
heavy tasks from spring to harvest;
the sack-cloth pilgrimages under rain

to repair the slabbery gaps of winter
with the labourer hibernating
in his cottage for half the year
to greet the indignity of the Hiring Fair.

Fewer hands, bigger markets, larger farms.
Yet something mourns. The iron-ribbed
lamp flitting through the yard at dark,
the hissing froth, and fodder scented warmth

of a wood stalled byre, or leather thong
of flail curling in a barn, were part
of a world where action had been wrung
through painstaking years to ritual.

Acknowledged when the priest blessed
the green tipped corn, or Protestant
lugged pale turnip, swollen marrow
to robe the kirk for Thanksgiving.

Palmer's softly lit Vale of Shoreham
commemorates it, or Chagall's lovers
floating above a childhood village
remote but friendly as Goldsmith's Auburn —

[82]

Our finally lost dream of man at home
in a rural setting! A giant hand
as we pass by, reaches down
to grasp the fields we gazed upon

Harsh landscape that haunts me,
well and stone, in the bleak moors of dream
with all my circling a failure to return
to what is already going

           going

                GONE

NOTES

NOTES

The Rough Field, adapted for reading and directed by Liam Miller (1924-87) was presented at the Peacock Theatre, Dublin, on 11 December 1972. The music, arranged by Paddy Moloney, was played by the Chieftains. The readers were Benedict Kiely, Tom McGurk, John Montague, and Alun Owen. On 8 July 1973, the British Irish Association presented a performance of this adaptation at the Round House in London, for which the readers were Seamus Heaney, Benedict Kiely, Tom McGurk, Patrick Magee, and John Montague. This performance was filmed by Radio Telefís Éireann and recorded for Claddagh Records, later issued as *An Ulster Epic: The Rough Field* (2001), CCT19–20 CD.

The illustrations on the cover and title page are details from John Derricke's *A Discoverie of Woodkarne* (see note 32). Captioned in doggerel verse, these twelve woodcut plates depict the Irish in Ulster and Sir Henry Sidney's campaigns against them, especially against Hugh O'Neill, in the 1570s. These woodcuts complement Derricke's seven-part poem *The Image of Irelande* (1581), which exaggerates the success of Sidney, then the English lord deputy in Ireland, in subduing the O'Neills and the Gaelic aristocracy of Ulster, after a three-year campaign, in 1578. *The Image of Irelande, with a Discoverie of Woodkarne, wherein is…expressed, the Nature…of the…Wilde Irishe Woodkarne, their notable aptnesse celeritie and pronesse to Rebellion*, as Derricke's title more fully runs, obviously describes the 'Wilde Irishe' from an English standpoint, but it also records contemporary Irish customs, dress, and methods of warfare. Among them are portraits of a harp-playing bard and another of an outlaw, or woodkerne from *ceithearnaigh coille* (*ceithearnaigh*, kern, or soldier; *coille*, wood), who wears the Irish cloak that became synonymous with Irish treachery. In 1985, Blackstaff Press, Belfast, published a facsimile of the 1883 edition of *The Image of Irelande*.

Title page: *The Rough Field* is English for the Irish *garbh acaidh*, anglicized as Garvaghey, the name of the County Tyrone townland where Montague was raised.

NOTES ON THE TEXT

These expanded notes have been adapted by the editors from Thomas Dillon Redshaw's revised annotations for this critical edition of *The Rough Field*.

10 *Orange and Legion Halls*: Neighborhood meeting halls of the Orange Order, founded in reaction to the Catholic Relief Act of 1793, and of the British Legion of ex-servicemen.

Royal Road: Also called the Lisburn Road (route A3), which runs from central Belfast southwest through Lisburn, Lurgan, Portadown, to Dungannon. It roughly divides Catholic Ulster to the west from Protestant Ulster to the east, an area comparable to the *Pale*, a region of English hegemony around Dublin, established by Richard II (1395), where English language, law, and customs prevailed. *O'Neill*, metonymically, was the opposite of the Pale, lands dominated by the O'Neills where the Irish language, Brehon law, and Gaelic customs endured until the Ulster Plantation (1608–1620).

11   *Ancient Order*: Founded in 1641, the Ancient Order of Hibernians was revived in 1838 to counter Orange opposition to Catholic Emancipation (1829) and later campaigned for Home Rule and, in the 1920s and 1930s, for Catholic civil rights in Northern Ireland.

Ulster's Volunteers: A Protestant militia led by Edward Carson and James Craig (1877–1940) which drilled openly against Home Rule, ran German guns into Ulster (1913), and became the Ulster Division of the British Army during World War I. Many of its veterans joined the Royal Ulster Constabulary (1919), sometimes as the "B-Specials." It was disbanded in 1966 by Terence O'Neill.

Hugh O'Neill: With Red Hugh O'Donnell (1572–1602), O'Neill (1545–1603) led the Northern Confederacy (1594–1613) against Dublin and Elizabeth I. He fled Ireland and died in Rome.

Lamh Dearg Abus: Irish for "Red Hand Forever," the battle cry of the O'Neills and the Northern Confederacy.

12   *Hedge schoolmaster*: In circumvention of the proscriptions of the Penal Laws (1695–1829) against education in Irish, towns and villages hired itinerant schoolmasters, often trained on the Continent, to teach in the houses of prosperous tenants or in their fields. See William Carleton's "The Hedge School" in *Traits and Stories of the Irish Peasantry* (1830).

Redmondite: A follower of John Redmond (1856–1918), leader of the Irish Parliamentary Party after Parnell who won passage of the Third Home Rule Bill (1912). His acceptance of the exclusion of the 'Six Counties' from that bill and his support of Irish conscription during World War I led to his electoral defeat by Sinn Féin in 1918.

post Famine years: The potato blight and famine (1845–49), which reduced Ireland's population by starvation and emigration from 9 to 6.5 million, led to agitation by tenants for land reform. Twelve land acts passed by Parliament between 1860 and 1904 eventually enabled Irish tenants to acquire legal title to the lands that they worked.

13 *Tague*: From *tadhg*, "poet," "philosopher," or "fool"; also a Christian name and an Orange epithet for a Catholic, as in "Lilliburlero" (1687).

Cardinal Manning: A convert from the Anglican church, Henry Edward Manning (1808–92) became archbishop of Westminster in 1865. A leading figure in Vatican I (1869–70), Manning espoused social, educational, and labor causes, especially those pertaining to Ireland.

Dagda: The 'Good God' of the druids and 'All Father' of the Tuatha Dé Danann, the Dagda of Irish myth is the corpulent landlord of the *sídhe* mounds and a provider whose cauldron of food can never be emptied by any hunger.

15 *King Billy*: With Queen Mary, William III reigned from 1688 to 1702. His victory over James II at the Boyne on July 1, 1690 made the image of William on his white horse an icon of Orange supremacy. His victory is celebrated by Orange lodges on 12 July in parades featuring the large lambeg drum, fifes, and the standard marching uniform of dark suits, orange sashes, furled umbrellas, and bowler hats.

Fomorian: A tribe of western demons, the Fomoire were defeated by the Tuatha Dé Danann at Moytura, as recounted in the twelfth-century *Leabhar Gabhála Éireann*.

17 *Brigid*: The goddess Brígh kept a vestal shrine at Knockaulin, County Kildare. Likewise, Saint Brigid of Kildare (d. 525) taught her nuns to guard a perpetual flame in an outdoor sanctuary.

18 *The Little Flower*: The sobriquet of Marie Françoise Thérèse Martin (1873–97), a Carmelite nun and author of *Histoire d'une âme* (1898), canonized in 1925 as Sainte Thérèse de Lisieux.

a family farm: Located above Garvaghey and under Slievemore on the Derry to Dublin road (route A5).

24 *The Prime Minister*: Harold Wilson, head of Britain's 1964–70 Labour government. This letter appeared in the *Belfast Newsletter*, 1 May 1967, and in other British and Irish newspapers. The *Treaty of Rome* (25 March 1957) established the European Economic Community (EEC), which the United Kingdom and the Republic of Ireland joined in 1973. The *Coronation Oath* binds a British monarch to "uphold the Protestant Faith."

25 *He who stood at midnight*: Excerpted from "The Midnight Mass" by William Carleton (1794–1856), in the second series of *Traits and Stories of the Irish Peasantry* (1833).

27 *ECUMENISM*: An Orange retort to the opening of Vatican II (11 October 1962) and to the encyclicals *Gaudet Mater Ecclesia* (1962) and *Pacem in Terris* (1963) of Pope John XXIII.

28 *LOYALISTS REMEMBER!*: The Irish Rising of 1641–50 occasioned the Protestant belief that Gaelic, Catholic supporters of Charles I had slaughtered Ulster Protestants. *Frog Queen Henrietta*, Henrietta Maria, sister of Louis XIII of France and wife of Charles I.

Roger Moore and Sir Phelim O'Neill: Roger or Rory O'Moore (1620–52) and Sir Phelim O'Neill (1604–53) rose in 1641 against the Parliamentarians governing in Dublin and founded the Catholic Confederation of Kilkenny (1642) loyal to Charles I.

Oliver Cromwell (1599–1658): Responded to Owen Roe O'Neill's 1646 victory at Benburb, County Tyrone, by occupying Dublin and then sacking Wexford and Drogheda, where his troops executed many Irish and Old English monarchists.

Altamuskin: One of the sites of open-air Masses held in Penal Times until as late as the 1870s in rural Ireland.

cousin: Protected by their Protestant landlords, in the eighteenth and early nineteenth centuries the Montagues tended the Altamuskin massrock, stored vestments, sheltered itinerant priests, and sent many of the men of their family into the priesthood.

29 *An Ulster Prophecy*: Adapted as a prophetic vision from a Gaelic "lying song" collected in Tyrone, ca. 1905.

Shankill: From *sean chill* ("old church"), a Protestant neighborhood on Shankill Road running west from the center of Belfast and parallel to Falls Road, from *fál* ("hedged enclosure"), a Catholic neighborhood.

The crest is that of the United Irishmen, founded in 1791 in Belfast by Theobald Wolfe Tone (1763–98). Intending to ally Presbyterians and Catholics on the rationalist terms of the French Revolution, the United Irishmen rose against British rule in Ireland in 1798. The quick suppression of this rising led to the 1800 Act of Union and to the insurrectionary tradition of Irish republicanism.

32 *Karne* or kerne: From *ceithearnaigh*, denoting Irish infantrymen serving local chiefs. The English used the term to mean "savages" or "wild men" who lived beyond the Pale.

Sir Thomas Phillips (1580–1620): Reported in detail the wealth of the lands around Derry for the London Company. Rev. George Hill quotes liberally from Phillips's correspondence in chapter eight of his *Historical Account of the Plantation in Ulster* (1877).

Salisbury: Sir Robert Cecil (1563–1612), chief administrator for Elizabeth I.

Sir John Davies: Letter of 1609 from Limavady, quoted in Hill's *Historical Account*, p. 169. Davies (1569–1626) later composed *A Discoverie of the True Causes Why Ireland was Never Entirely Subdued until the Beginning of His Majesty's Reign* (1612).

33 *sally switch*: Fashioned from the cane of the willow or *saileach*.

34 *ceannbhán*: Bog Cotton. The literal Irish translation is "white head."

sleán: A narrow spade used for cutting turves out of a bog.

Golden Stone or *Cloch Óir*: Anglicized as Clogher, a diocesan town south of Ballygawley near the birthplace of William Carleton.

homesick poem: William Carleton's "A Sigh for Knockmany," published in Dublin's *National Magazine* (April, 1831).

35 *Rapparee*: From *rapaire*, "robber." The first to bear this name were disbanded, Jacobite soldiers who continued guerilla attacks after 1691. *Shane Barnagh*, a local and legendary Robin Hood of the late eighteenth century, was a rapparee.

Brish-mo-Cree: A popular expression, anglicized from *Bris mo chroí*, meaning "my heart breaks."

Tá an Ghaeilge againn arís: "We have the Irish again."

O'Hagans: The Ó hÁgáin family traditionally conducted the inauguration of the O'Neill at Tullyhogue. The coronation stone there was destroyed by Mountjoy in 1602.

gallowglasses: From *gallóglaich*, dating from the thirteenth century and denoting mercenary soldiers from Scotland, such as the MacDonnells or MacSweenys, who served the O'Donnells and settled in Antrim and Donegal.

Kinsale: A town in County Cork, where a famous battle occurred on 24 December 1601, ending Hugh O'Neill's long campaign against the Elizabethan Plantation and ensuring both the collapse of Gaelic Ireland and the inevitability of English settlement.

Sir George Carew (1555–1629): Lord president of Munster and antiquarian.

Con Bacach O'Neill, 1542: A supporter of the rebellion of Silken Thomas, Con "the Lame" O'Neill (1484–1559) took English titles but repeatedly invaded the Pale.

36 *Sean an Diomas, 1562*: "Shane the Proud" O'Neill (1530–67) submitted to Elizabeth I in 1562. An opponent of the O'Donnells, Shane O'Neill was murdered in 1567 at Cushendun. His death enabled Sir Henry Sidney to extend the Elizabethan Plantation into central Ulster.

Hugh O'Neill, 1599: An ally of Sidney, despite having eloped with Margaret Bagenal, Hugh O'Neill (1550–1616) began to forge his Northern Confederacy against Dublin after he became both head of the O'Neills ("the O'Neill") and Earl of Tyrone in 1595. O'Neill's victory over Sir Henry Bagenal at the Yellow Ford (1598) confirmed his leadership of Gaelic, Catholic Ireland.

Sir John Harrington: Translator of Ariosto's *Orlando Furioso* (1591). Harrington (1561–1612) campaigned in Ireland, visited O'Neill, and held title to lands in County Armagh.

38 *Annals of the Four Masters*: This description of the 'Flight of the Earls' appears in the *Annals of the Kingdom of Ireland* by the Four Masters, translated from the Irish by John O'Donovan (1856).

Chichester: Sir Arthur Chichester (1563–1625), lord deputy of Ireland and the chief architect of the Ulster plantation. See Cyril Falls, *Elizabeth's Irish Wars* (1970), p. 277.

Mountjoy: Sir Charles Blount (1563–1606), eighth Lord Mountjoy and Earl of Devonshire, lord deputy of Ireland (1599–1603). Mountjoy accepted O'Neill's submission to Elizabeth I on 30 March 1603—days after her death. He then accepted O'Neill's submission to James I on 6 April, granting O'Neill his English titles on 17 April.

39 *bardic poem*: "*Anocht is uaigneach Éire*," by Annrias Mac Marcuis, on the 'Flight of the Earls' (1607).

Lough Swilly: Between Donegal and Derry, from which the O'Neills and the O'Donnells sailed in 1607 into exile on the Continent.

40 *Names twining braid Scots and Irish*: Eighteen mostly Tyrone placenames stud these five stanzas, each evoking a moment in Ulster's settlement. For example, *Ania's Cove* on Knockmany and *Sess Kill Green* near Ballygawley are names of Neolithic passage graves. *Routing Burn* and *Bloody Brae* are names of Scots origin. *Fall Brae* combines Irish (*fál*, "enclosure") with Scots dialect (*brá*, "brow," originally from the Norse). *New Town Civil* or Saville west of Garvaghey; *Favour Royal* or Moyenner (1611), east of Augher; and *Spur Royal* (1615), west of Augher, are names of Planter estates.

42 *Dr. Patrick McCartan May 1916*: A doctor from Carrickmore, County Tyrone, and leader of the Irish Republican Brotherhood, McCartan (1878–1966) worked in Philadelphia on the behalf of Irish nationalism, served as de Valéra's envoy to both President Wilson and Lenin (1918–20), voted for the Anglo-Irish Treaty of 1921, and later ran for president of the Free State.

Winston Churchill 1922: Speaking in the House of Commons, 16 February 1922. Churchill moved the Irish Free State Bill, which recognized Liam Cosgrave's government as the Saorstát Éireann. *Winston Churchill: His Complete Speeches, 1897–1963*, ed. R. R. James (1974).

46 *I.R.T.*: The Interborough Rapid Transit subway line, which runs up through New York City.

48 *Che Guevara*: Attributed to the Latin American revolutionary during his campaign in Bolivia by Richard N. Goodwin, in *The New Yorker* (25 May 1968).

To say a song: In Irish, *amhrán a rá*, the invitation traditionally made to a *sean nós* or 'old style' singer to perform.

49 *An Bunnán Buí*: "The Yellow Bittern," by Cathal Buí Mac Giolla Ghunna (1680–1756), in which the thirsty poet or singer uses a bittern, found dead, as a metaphor for his own condition.

51 *Erne base*: During World War II, the Royal Air Force moored at Castle Archdale, a Planter estate on Lower Lough Erne, squadrons of Sunderlands and Catalinas, 'flying boats' used to hunt German submarines and escort North Atlantic convoys.

52 *ancient trout of wisdom*: The hero Fionn Mac Cumhaill received his adult name and the three arts of poetry—prophecy, divination, and "incantation from heads"—by catching and cooking this fish, which was fed by nuts dropped from the hazels of wisdom into a well called Linn Féicc. Fionn sucked his thumb after burning it on the fish's flesh and then extemporaneously composed the fourteen measures of the poem "Cétemain" ("Fionn's Poem on May Day"). After that, Fionn could call upon his wisdom (*eolas*) simply by putting his thumb in his mouth.

54 *showbands*: Excerpted from an article in the *Evening Press* (Dublin), 29 July 1967, p. 8.

   Sir John's: Also called Ballygawley Park, a Big House of the Stewart family, burned during the Troubles of the 1920s.

60 *by Glencull Waterside*: A newspaper ballad by Patrick Farrell, reprinted for a dedication program of the Cardinal McRory Memorial Park (1956). *Glencull* is an Anglicization of *Gleann chuil*, "Glen of the Hazels."

63 *Seán Ó Riada* (1931–71): Musicologist and composer, founder of *Ceoltóirí Chualann*, from which the Chieftains emerged, and leader of the popular renaissance of traditional Irish music.

64 *1916 Room*: An exhibition in Kilmainham Gaol, Dublin, displaying memorabilia of the leaders of the Easter Rising, 24–29 April 1916.

65 *smell of appleblossom*: W. B. Yeats, *The Autobiography* (1965), p. 82; *luckless luck*, pp. 57–58.

   mauser gun: Used Mauser rifles were run into Howth Harbor, 26 July 1914, on the Asgard and then distributed to the Irish Volunteers, which became the Irish Republican Army in 1919.

   Connolly's dream: The Worker's Republic, as envisioned by James Connolly (1868–1916), the Marxist ally of James Larkin (1876–1947) in the Dublin lock-out of 1913, and commandant of the General Post Office during the Easter Rising.

66 *Máirtín Ó Cadhain* (1907–1970): Member of the Irish Republican Army in the 1930s and 1940s, Irish language scholar, and novelist noted for *Cré na Cille* (1949).

The Enterprise: Formerly the name of the express passenger train running between Belfast and Dublin.

67 *Coole Park*: The Big House of Lady Augusta Gregory (1852–1932), which was demolished by the local council in 1941. The initials carved into the *beech-tree* include those of Sean O'Casey, George Russell (AE), George Bernard Shaw, and W. B. Yeats.

68 *Vatican*: Before the opening of Vatican II, Pope John XXIII received Queen Elizabeth II, titular head of the Church of England, in an audience on 6 May 1961.

trade expansion of 5 per cent: Supported by Taoiseach Seán Lemass (1899–1971), T. K. Whitaker (b. 1916) laid the foundation for Ireland's economic development programs of 1958–72.

Fleadh Cheoil: Literally "feast of music," a national festival of traditional music, this one held in Mullingar in 1963.

69 *Pope John:* Pope John XXIII died on Whitmonday, 3 June 1963.

70 *Skelligs*: From the Irish *na Scealaga* ("the Splinters"), a group of craggy islets off the coast of County Kerry, including Skellig Michael, a Christian hermitage. *Hy Brasil*, a magical island in the Atlantic protected by the sea-god Manannán mac Lir.

71 *Bernadette Devlin* (b. 1947): An early advocate of Catholic civil rights active in Derry and a frequently jailed M.P. for Mid-Ulster (1969–74).

Catholic quarter: The Bogside or Creggan Estate in Derry.

72 *Roaring Meg*: One of the cannons used by Rev. George Walker's Protestant garrison to fend off Maréchal de Rosen's Jacobite troops during the Siege of Londonderry (18 April–31 July, 1689).

SMALL SHOT: Excerpted from Rev. Seth Whittle, "A Sermon Preached before the Garrison of London-Derry in the Extremity of the Siege."

the slain Irish: From Rev. George Walker, *The Siege of Londonderry in 1689*, ed. Dwyer (1893), p. 36.

"No Surrender": This Unionist and Orange rallying cry descends from 7 December 1688 when Derry's apprentices locked Ferry Quay Gate against Lord Deputy Tyrconnell's Catholic regiment representing James II.

a black Cuchulain: The Rev. Ian Paisley (b. 1926), Free Presbyterian minister, representative to the European Parliament (1979), and a champion of fundamentalism and right-wing Unionism, called "Cuchulain" here after the mythical champion of Ulster in the *Táin Bó Cúailnge*.

73 *man dove*: A scion of the O'Neill family, St. Columba or Columcille (521–97), from *Choluim Chille* ("Dove of the Church"), resisted the interference of the Gaelic princes in church affairs, resulting in the Battle of Culdremna (561), after which Columcille settled Iona and undertook his mission to Scotland.

ledge of angels: From a poem attributed to Columcille.

Lir's white daughter's: The enchantment of Fionnuala and her brothers, who were metamorphosed into white swans by their stepmother Aoife in *Oidheadh Chlainne Lir*, ended at Columcille's Convention of Druim Cett (575), when a woman of the South married a man of the North.

is uaigneach Eire: See note for page 39 on *bardic poem*.

London's Derry: Fortified by Henry Docwra (d. 1613) in 1600, then granted to the citizens of London by James I in 1613, Derry and its hinterland were planted by twelve London guilds organized together as the Honourable Irish Society, otherwise called the London Company.

DIDOE'S COLONY: A passage excerpted from a letter to Sir Robert Cecil in which Sir John Davies lauds the founding of Coleraine (1613). See Hill, p. 406.

O'Cahan, O' Doherty: Sir Cahir Ua Dochartaigh (1587–1608) was beheaded after rising against Derry and then Lord Chichester. Implicated in the rising, Sir Donnell Ballagh ("the Freckled") O'Cahan was imprisoned in the Tower of London, where he died in 1617.

Lundy slides: Governor of Derry, Robert Lundy (d. 1717) fled the town at the start of the siege.

ORANJE BOVEN!: "Orange Forever!", the battle cry of Dutch Williamite forces.

74 *Burntollet*: In a civil rights march from Belfast to Derry, 1–4 January 1969, members of the People's Democracy movement were attacked at Burntollet Bridge, which led to riots in Derry's Bogside and the start of what came to be known as 'the Northern Troubles'.

75 *Carson's*: The statue of Sir Edward Carson (1854–1935), leader of the Irish Unionist Party at Westminster (1910–21) and creator of the Ulster Volunteer Force (1911), stands in front of Stormont, the parliament of Northern Ireland.

captain that: Captain Terence O'Neill (1914–90) and his cousin Major James Chichester-Clark (b. 1923) were prime ministers of Northern Ireland during 1963–69 and 1969–71 respectively.

blue banner: The Plough-and-Stars flag of Connolly and Larkin's labor movement.

DRIVE YOUR PLOUGH: See William Blake's *The Marriage of Heaven and Hell* (1792), pl. 7, 1.2.

THE RELIEF SHIP: Adapted from Macaulay's *A History of England* (1848–61), in which the dramatic account of the Siege of Londonderry ensured the siege's heroic status in Irish political legend. Towed in a dead calm under hostile fire, Kirke's flagship *Mountjoy* crossed the Jacobite boom at Culmore on the Foyle estuary and relieved Walker's garrison on 28 July 1689.

78 *cailleach*: Irish and Scots Gaelic for an old woman, hag, or nun.

82 *Palmer's…Vale of Shoreham*: Near Sevenoaks, Kent, from which the English painter and engraver Samuel Palmer, a member of William Blake's circle, drew his pastoral idealizations of seasonal village life.

December, 2004